AF374172

Dedication

To my mother, who has always seen me through the darkness.

And my son, who I pray will find his own strength and serenity.

To those who have been in my corner...

THANK YOU:

To my husband for the reminders that words are the tether to my heart.

To my mom for the coffee dates and the second pair of eyes to parse through it all.

To Bethany for constant encouragement and affirmation of worthiness.

To Savannah for working side by side toward a common goal.

And to Katie, without whom this would still be a document on my computer.

Table of Contents

Regenesis

Write

because without words
we are no better
than the inanimate
objects we observe

Prodigal

Closing time

I sit in a mess of half-finished journals: a composition book that starts with my first lost tooth, and stops with my first lost love; mini pocket journals about a forgotten love deemed unforgettable; the "heartbreak journal" detailing thoughts of self-harm and suicide after losing love and loved-ones, and all the mess that sits in between.

These pages contain evidence of a pain scattered linearly behind me and yet so acutely tethered to the way I see life now. They tell me that I was doomed to fail; that my heart would break me down until I had nothing. And maybe that's why revisiting is so uncomfortable... because that girl did fail, and I'm just now coming to terms with her death. So, I'm ready for one last goodbye. I'm ready to accept that my past has lived and died.

Distance

Never knowing

Where are you
these days?
she asked me
with only two cups
of coffee between us.
Sometimes,
never knowing
is a blessing
and a curse.

Words won't do

they say words won't do–
that a picture is worth
a thousand of them,
but no picture can capture
the gentle tenderness
of your fingers entwined
effortlessly within mine;
even a picture can never say
the words of comfort you spoke
from a thousand miles away;
and a picture can't duplicate
the warmth of your body
as you hold me tight.

I heart bacon

there are thousands of words
in the english dictionary
and yet
we have somehow fallen into
the trap of explaining how
we feel about people
with the same words we use
to explain how we feel
about our favorite foods.
this morning I told you
how much I love bacon,
but tonight you will tell me
how much you love
me

21st century "i miss you"

I start to feel the curse
of technology as I watch
the distance from me to you
steadily increase
moment by moment–
as if how much i miss you
can now be described
as an observable ever-growing,
concretely numerical value;
not just the abstract pain
of slowly forgetting
the exact hue of your eyes,
smell of your skin,
or the feel of your hand in mine.

The silent argument

How is it that,
with zero communication,
and hundreds of miles
between us,
I can still feel
the weight of this argument
with every cycle of
silent emotion?
I don't need you here
to tell me
the plethora of ways
in which I am failing.
I can feel myself deflating
as I watch the box of tissues
slowly dwindle down
to nothing.

Never let me

never let me make your life harder.
never let me push you into a corner.
never let me make you choose
between one thing you love and another.
never let me wake you up
if you're meant to be a dreamer.

and if i ever do, never let me stay.

Summer storms

I used to love to watch you
light up like the night's sky
on the distant horizon
during a summer storm.
Your magnificence
is a thing to behold,
but only
from the safest of distances.

Lost
in translation

Sometimes I lie
awake at night
wondering what
my life would look like
if nothing had been lost
in translation.
If your mouth
and my ears
had been opened.
If you had heard.
If I had spoken.

In the glove box

it's easier to forget your last mistake
when you're already so wrapped up
in your next misstep;
living life in the midst of wrong turns,
never pausing to ask
for directions,
or to decide which heading
actually makes sense–
as long as these memories
are stored somewhere
deep in the glove box.

Revisit

do you remember
when we said
we'd wait a few years
and then we'd see where
we stood?
well, here you are
standing in the vestibule,
cracking open the door
we shut so forcefully
years ago.
as i stand at the threshold
looking back into your world
so comfortingly familiar,
yet so different from my own
i can't help but wonder
what time is telling me
to do today.

Game of jacks

this time
when i jumped
my heart hit the floor
in such a way
that it spilled everything.
all the fractured pieces
from the past scattered
like a million jacks
made of bundles of scar tissue
on the hardwood floor.
each time the ball bounces
i pick up a different piece
of my past,
reliving those memories
and begging
for no more scars.
this time
when i reassemble my heart
i can't help but wonder
if there's anything left
to hold it together.

Temptation

My story

Today I will tell them my story
that 1 in 5 women can tell–
I will tell them because my pen dries up
when I try to write it all down.

As I stared at my wounds on the paper,
all I could do was wonder what pain
my story would cause them,
if they knew the aching inside of me.

As I speak I see clearly:
I know all is well within me;
I see His Love all around me.

Victim

and now that you've walked
out of my life,
i carefully select my next victim—
never realizing
that it will always be me

Statistic

The red hue of the earth seeped away,
and blue sky melted into grey clouds.
I felt my soul wither within me,
and my dignity die with it.

I had become another number.

Symbiotic failure

you used me
to feed your loneliness,
and i hoped you'd heal
my heartache,
but here we sit
in a twisted torment
wondering who was left
more bruised

Branded

sometimes all I want
is to go back
to when my innocence hit
the crossroads of
your brand
and my mother's expectations

Intoxicated

You say I'm a fantastic idea,
but only when intoxicated–
as if allowing yourself to give in
to just one more thing
isn't such a big deal
when you're already drowning
in your other indulgences–
but maybe you're afraid
of getting addicted
to one more substance, forgetting that I'm
the only thing of true substance;
maybe you're afraid
of coming off my high,
forgetting that this high won't crash,
so long as you keep flying
with the wings I've tried to give.

Our innocence

Your words picked at the edge
of my conscience
and stuck on the tip of my tongue–
but I wanted
to try them out for myself: "You whore."

You're the one who branded me
with this scarlet letter of shame
to pass off the responsibility because
I fell too easily. Again.

No matter how many nights I lie
awake, wishing each tear that slipped
silently to the pillow was meant
to release me from this torment, you and I
are a history forever engrained,
like an etch-a-sketch
I can't shake away.

But I choose not
to fight your memory anymore,
because this is not between you and me,
but beyond you and me.

This is a war that started
with Adam and Eve;
A war against animalistic nature,
to be fought side by side
–not throat to throat–
until the blame gets wrapped up
in the indignant ache we hold in
and swallow like a polite guest
at an all too fancy dinner.

To start this war, I forgive you
and beg pardon.
But to end, I'll need to forgive myself.

Phoenix from
the ashes

I was mistaken in my assessment of you,
and I spread lies of your character
like wildfire on a windy day–
how do you go back from a scar
quite like that?
Each lie a tongue of fire
licking the earth
and charring its surface,
until completely unrecognizable
to the untrained eye.
But I do know you,
and I see you lift up from the ashes
like a rising phoenix
baptized by fire;
innocent in your youth reborn.
The chaff of your soul
consumed by the very flames
I scarred your reputation with.

Whole
as the day

Thank you for reminding me that today I am
as whole as the day.

–as the day Nani died, depression grabbed hold,
or thoughts of suicide came knocking.
–as the days I didn't ask for it, was branded
"you whore," or "no" froze on my lips.
–as the days I can take a deep breath because
I have found peace.

The same today as yesterday: forever whole.

Daughter

Found

I knew I found Love
when the sorrows of my past
dissolved into joy.

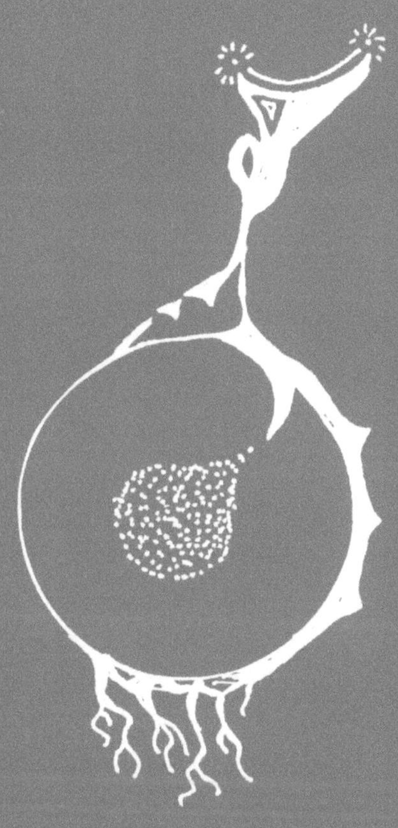

Becoming

You were right

and now
there's a newness
to us—
a fresh innocence,
a pure friendship—
i feel so much more
myself without you
always on my mind.
there's a freedom
in this mutual agreement
to just be friends.
so, thank you
for showing me
that this woman can
be wrong.

Date night

i took myself out
on a date tonight–
flip flops and a bro tank
because there's no one left
to impress–
my charm is good enough
for me.
even if there was someone
beside me on this bluff,
this sunset would look
no more beautiful.

Twitterpated

there's something about
this crisp mountain air
that makes the heart beat
a little faster,
the eyes catch hold
of some flightless beauty,
the feet step quicker
toward the open potential—
as if thinner air
means less to wade through;
there's a clear line of sight
toward what actually matters.

Amp

I lie, limbs sprawling unladylike
across the queen sized bed.
I feel my body pulse in an unfamiliar way;
as if my chest had acquired a second heart
and the veins of a life worth living.

As I fall asleep

I am on a different planet–
an alternate sphere,
a reciprocated mode of thought–
as I slip into this blissful euphoria
and sail through space and time
on wings made of cotton sheets;
my consciousness skips across
clouds of rapture like rocks on a pond.

Depth of clouds

i love the sky
when it rains
on a dark night
and the only thing
to remind us of its depth
are the sudden bursts of light
embedded in the night's clouded sky

Gods in the sky

It's no wonder the ancients believed in gods
when the sky hangs thick with humidity
and pulls each of your hairs on edge.
You can see the deamons clashing–
feel each blow of airborne warfare
in the awesomeness of an electrified sky.

Colors of the sky

when i'm with you
i appreciate every moment
the way i appreciate watching the sun
as it falls
beneath the horizon–

each moment is full
of deep reflection and serenity,
but also ripe
with excitement
and unending potential–

there is an openness
to this beauty,
an inevitability
to the richness of color;
as if we are simply

a light destined to shine.

With the anonymous you

there is
an indescribable beauty
wrapped up
in the stacks of photographs,
in the piles of
unpublished
and unprofessional work—
something raw
and exhilarating
in the subtle reminders
that there is passion
and love
here
in this life, and i
have been blessed enough
to witness it
and feel it

Found

Discover the me in you

to love someone
is to walk
side by side–
to admire the other
in their separate beauty
while growing complete
in your own;
but to be in love
is to walk
arm in arm–
to admire the self
you find in the other,
becoming complete
in this self-discovery

Float for you

I've forgotten
what it feels like
to fall in love.
It's not the loving part
that I am incapable of,
it's the falling part
that scares me the most.
But when I find
the right one,
I know it will feel
like floating.

jump.

our ability to love
is only as strong
as our ability
to push away fear
of heartbreak–
our ability to recognize
nothing is perfect
but sometimes
we just have to
take a breath
and

jump.

Blow me away

you came at me
like wind across the water,
I could not feel you yet,
but I could see
the powerful disturbance
your presence makes.
curious fingertips reaching out
along the water,
leaving ripples in their wake.

and now that you've hit me,
I can feel your fingers
through my hair,
leaving me a tangled, happy mess,
ready to live life
with the top down,
sun glasses on,
and my hands in your breeze.

Out of body

I don't recognize
these corridors in my mind;
where does this lead to?

Pause

Take a breath–a pause;
allow yourself one moment
purely for the soul.

Perfectly present

I am done dreaming;
nothing could even compare
to reality.

Jigsaw

God love this messy
jigsaw puzzle; have mercy
on our pretty pieces

When I met you

you held your long limbed body
in a way that told me you owned it–
a way that told me you understood it,
a way that didn't scream
or shout,
or yell,
but firmly stated the fact that you exist.

Used to you

I got used to you
on a rooftop under
the autumn night sky.
Each story warmed me up,
as if every single
spontaneous fragment
of your being
could find a home
in each of the
complex cavities in my heart,
until all my dark
and mysterious corners
were set on fire
by your contagious,
windblown flames
to illuminate
our perfect puzzle.

Sanctioned knowledge

I want to know you
by the curve in your back
and the way it should feel
to find my body
encompassed by yours.

I want to know you
by the length of your spine
and the way it should feel
to wrap my arms
around your sturdy form.

I want to know you
at the base of your frame
and the way it should feel
to love someone
from the marrow in your bones.

Coast

I spent my day at the ocean
with my eyes stuck on my feet,
and my mind stuck in midair–
a kite adrift in the breeze.

Riding thermals

The search is over:
I know this by
the feeling of floating
with no other purpose
but to exist by your side
and observe you as we are
drifting,
dancing,
dreaming–
together riding the thermals
of a life forever in flux.

Now

There's a beautiful gift the now brings;
a peace that comes when expected good is realized;
a comfort that washes over when uncovered light

> shines through the darkness.

www.ingramcontent.com/pod-product-compliance
Lightning Source LLC
Chambersburg PA
CBHW040913110726
48005CB00006B/873